THE MINI ROUGH GUIDE TO
Turkey

D0813212

ROUGH
GUIDES

roughguides.com

Credits

Editor: Ian Blenkinsop
Picture research: Diana Jarvis
Design & layout: Diana Jarvis
Cartography: Ed Wright
Proofreader: Stewart Wild
Production: Gemma Sharpe
Project manager (Rough Guides): Ian Blenkinsop
Project manager (Redmint Communications): Ceyda Sara Pekenç-Gürer
Account manager (Rough Guides): Michael Stanfield
Director of Turkish Culture & Tourism Office: Tolga Tüylüoğlu

Published 2012 by Rough Guides Ltd, 80 Strand, London WC2R 0RL

© Rough Guides Ltd, 2012

Printed in the UK by Ashford Colour Press

ISBN 978 1 40932 506 2

MIX
Paper from
responsible sources
FSC® C011748

Contents

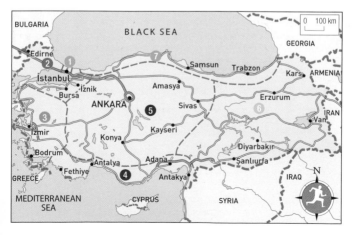

Introduction

With its unique mix of the exotic and the familiar, visiting Turkey can be a mesmerizing experience. More than the "bridge between East and West" of tourist-brochure cliché, the country combines influences from the **Middle East** and the **Mediterranean**, the **Balkans** and **central Asia**. Invaded and settled from every direction since the start of recorded history, its contradictions and fascinations persist. Mosques coexist with churches, Roman theatres and temples crumble not far from ancient Hittite cities and dervish ceremonies or gypsy festivals are as much a part of the social landscape as classical music concerts or avidly attended football matches.

Another facet of Turkey that makes it such a rewarding place to travel is the **Turkish people**, whose reputation for friendliness and hospitality is richly deserved; indeed you risk causing offence by declining invitations and find yourself making friends through the simplest of transactions.

Turkey's rich **history** is a major draw for tourists, and the whole country is scattered with archaeological remains of the myriad civilisations that have blossomed and faded here across the centuries, and many excellent museums exist to interpret the country's complex past.

Turkey's **beaches** are perhaps its most famous asset and it's still entirely possible to find quiet coves and dramatic scenery among the resorts that punctuate the Aegean and Mediterranean coastlines. But **inland Turkey** – Asiatic expanses of mountain, steppe, lake, even cloud-forest – may leave even more vivid memories, especially when accented by some ancient monastery, mosque or castle.

<< COASTLINE NEAR ALANYA

Historic Sites and Museums

In terms of physical attractions, a huge part of Turkey's appeal lies in its archaeological sites, a legacy of the bewildering succession of states – Hittite, Urartian, Phrygian, Hellenistic, Roman, Byzantine – that held sway here before the twelfth century. From grand Classical cities to hilltop fortresses and remote churches, some still produce exciting new finds today. There is also, of course, a vast number of graceful Islamic monuments dating from the eleventh century onwards.

Given this depth of history, it's perhaps unsurprising that you're rarely far from a museum in Turkey. Some of the collections rank among the finest in the world and it's a treat to simply marvel at the ancient art, architecture and treasures on display, but with some well-chosen visits you can really get to grips with the country's rich past.

Ancient Ephesus

opposite; page 36

This ancient city, where St Paul addressed one of his epistles, is the best preserved of its kind in the Eastern Mediterranean.

Acropolis of Ancient Pergamon

Extensive ruins remain of one of the chief ancient Greek cities in Anatolia.

Kariye Museum

above left

Arguably the finest collection of mosaics and frescoes in Turkey, adorning a late-Byzantine church in İstanbul.

Museum of Anatolian Civilisations

page 47

Houses finds from all native cultures, from the Stone Age to about late antiquity; a must-see if you're in Ankara.

Nemrut Dağı

below left; page 53

This megalomaniac hilltop temple-tomb complex is the outlandish legacy of an obscure first-century BC kingdom.

Beaches

Few countries can boast as many fine beaches as Turkey, and for many visitors the sun, sea and sand are the principal attractions. Though some resort towns have grown rapidly in recent years, with over three hundred blue flag beaches strung along Turkey's coastlines, you're rarely far from a quiet stretch of sand and clean waters.

The Aegean coast is, in many ways, Turkey's most enticing destination, as a visit can easily combine some of the country's best antiquities with its most appealing resorts. If you head a little way off the beaten track, unspoilt seaside villages, clear seas and welcoming guesthouses are yours for the taking. At the Mediterranean, the "Turquoise Coast" begins; road access is impossible along much of the coast and consequently yacht and *gulet* trips are popular ways to appreciate the beauty of the region. A number of outstanding beaches – Patara and İztuzu among them – remain protected and untouched thanks to the endangered loggerhead turtles that nest there. Further east, the Mediterranean meets some of Turkey's most rugged coastline, but there are still plenty of great beaches, such as those around Anamur.

Uzunkum

Meaning "long sand", this beach near Ünye is one of the Black Sea Coast's finest strands; avoid swimming when the sea's rough though.

Konyaaltı Beach

right

The busy seaside centrepiece of the international resort city of Antalya on the Mediterranean Sea; a long pebble beach with awards for cleanliness.

Ölüdeniz
above; page 41

An azure lagoon on the Turquoise Coast, fringed by what are probably the most photographed beaches in Turkey.

Kaputaş Beach
left

Trapped between steep cliffs, the bright waters and golden sand of this tiny beach attract visitors from miles around, and passengers from tour boats.

Kıyıköy
Page 29

The two kilometres of sandy beach near this pretty, walled village on the Black Sea are backed by low cliffs, oozing fossils.

Turkish Cuisine

The amazing variety of Turkish food and drink is a direct link to its multilayered history. Here you'll find everything from rustic central Asian country cooking to the highly refined, Arab-inspired cuisine of the Ottoman court. At its finest, Turkish food is among the best in the world – indeed it is sometimes ranked alongside French and Chinese as one of the three classic cuisines. The quality of produce is reliably exceptional, with most ingredients being sourced locally; it's a good idea to ask what's in season during your visit, to get the best of what's on offer. There are too many mouth-watering national, regional and local specialities by far to mention them all, but here are a few common treats to look out for.

Baklava

Of all the myriad syrup-soaked baklava items on display, one of the best is *antep fıstıklı sarması*, which is filled with pistachio. *Künefe* – filaments of *kadayıf* vermicelli, perched atop white cheese, baked then soaked in syrup – has become similarly ubiquitous.

Meze

Appetisers for which Turkey is justly famous. Up to thirty kinds may be featured at licensed restaurants or *meyhanes*, comprising rich purées, vinaigrettes and the fried-then-chilled vegetarian dishes known as *zeytinyağlılar*.

Gözleme

A delicious snack of paper-thin dough stuffed with everything from spinach and sheep's cheese to lamb; watching their concoction is part of the fun.

Seafood

Turks all around the coast have always adored seafood, but the main focus is on the Bosphorus, where migrating species spark rounds of gastronomic indulgence each spring and autumn. Inland, trout (*alabalık*) and catfish (*yayın*) are commonly on the menu.

Helva

The recipe for the quintessential Turkish sweet, made from flour, butter, sugar and sometimes milk or starch, hasn't changed since it was first written down in 1473, and there are now countless different types on offer.

Natural Beauty

Turkey boasts one of the world's most exciting topographies. Spectacular alpine mountain ranges parallel both the azure waters of the Mediterranean and the storm-tossed Black Sea. Inland the vast uplands of ancient Anatolia are studded with volcanic peaks and sliced through by surging rivers, culminating in the 5000m bulk of legendary Mount Ararat, long thought to be the peak where Noah's ark came to rest. In Cappadocia, weirdly sculpted pinnacles stand like sentinels in a landscape reminiscent of the old Wild West.

Kaçkar Dağları
left; pages 54 & 61
Lying just inland from the Black Sea, this glacially sculpted granite mountain range, spangled with dozens of lakes, is a beautiful haven for trekkers.

Patara beach
page 43
This unspoilt beach, one of the longest in the Mediterranean, is the perfect coda to a visit of the nearby, eponymous ancient city.

Lake Van
page 57
The cobalt blue expanse of Lake Van, Turkey's largest, is most scenic in late spring or early summer.

Cappadocia
left; page 50

One of the country's star attractions, both for its unique landscapes of fairy chimneys and valleys, eroded from the soft tufa stone, and for its fascinating history of human settlement.

The Turquoise Coast
below; page 40

Turkey's southwesternmost shore, famed for its particularly fine beaches and stunning scenery, takes its name from the hues of its horizons and seas. A cruise aboard a traditional *gulet* is one of the best ways to take it all in.

Shopping

It's almost impossible to return from Turkey without some kind of souvenir; even if you're not a shopper by nature, the varied and unusual selection of gifts found in Turkey's markets – from packets of exotic spices to elegant carpets and kilims – is guaranteed to tempt you. The grand shops and teeming streets of İstanbul are a world away from the ateliers and craft shops of smaller towns in rural areas, and away from the city bustle, shopping is generally a much more relaxed pursuit. Covered bazaars – essentially medieval Ottoman shopping malls – are found in larger towns and cities and are an evocative place to browse and shop. The once- or twice-weekly street markets are a unique aspect of regional shopping in most towns, holdovers from the days of trading caravans when permanent shops did not exist. Bargaining is a way of life in the bazaars and markets and it's generally acceptable, even expected, to haggle over the price of souvenirs, which often lack price tags.

Carpets and Kilims

Turkish carpets and kilims (flat-weave rugs) are renowned for their quality and have a very long history. They're the quintessential Turkish souvenir and you're likely to find yourself in a carpet shop at some point in your trip.

Jewellery

In terms of design, quality and price, Turkey is a fantastic place to buy jewellery. Gold, silver and semi-precious stones are sold by weight – with little regard for the disparate levels of craftsmanship involved.

Local delicacies

Delicious sweets like helva, Turkish delight (*lokum*) and baklava are common purchases, and a wide array of fragrant spices, dried fruits and nuts are sold loose by weight in markets throughout Turkey.

Musical instruments

Traditional Turkish instruments are available almost everywhere. The most easily portable are the *ney* (Mevlevî flute), the *davul* (drum) and the *saz* (a long-necked lute).

Ceramics

Ceramics are an important artistic tradition in Turkey. The style varies according to the area of origin: İznik, Kütahya and Çanakkale are famous for ceramic production and Avanos is known for hand-painted pottery and porcelain.

Outdoor Adventure

Turkey's geographical and climatic diversity presents almost limitless possibilities for outdoor enthusiasts. Its mountain ranges and Anatolian winters are ideal for skiers and mountaineers, and the long, hot Mediterranean summers are perfect for yacht cruises, diving, windsurfing and a host of watersports. Spring and autumn are fairly short but the temperate conditions make them ideal for walking and cycling – activities that have really taken off here in recent years. Whatever you're into, make the most of these fabulous land- and seascapes: get off that sunbed and get active.

Hiking

Turkey's wild mountain ranges such as the Kaçkar are a treat for experienced walkers, and in southwest Mediterranean Turkey two long-distance paths – the Lycian Way and the St Paul Trail – take in magnificent natural scenery and offer a unique insight into rural Turkish life.

Rafting

Whitewater rafting has taken off in a big way in southwest Turkey. The Köprülü river near Antalya and the Dalaman river close to Fethiye are a thrilling introduction for novices. In the northeast, Çoruh offers world-class rapids, up to grade five.

Canyoning

Ideal for the congenitally active in the hot summer months; you can explore the wet, shady depths of spectacular gorges such as Saklıkent, Kaputaş or Kıbrıs in the Lycian mountains. Many resorts now offer one-day (or more) excursions – a perfect break from the beach.

Paragliding

Few activities combine the serenity and high-altitude scenery of paragliding. Babadağ Mountain, above Ölüdeniz (see p.41), and the mountain ridge above Kaş (see p.42) both have ideal updraughts, vistas and landing pads for this breathtaking sport.

Skiing

Turkey has a number of small but rapidly developing ski resorts that seem almost unknown to foreigners. Palandöken, in the northeast, has the best conditions and longest season, but other good options include Mount Erciyes, Uludağ, Kartalkaya, Saklıkent or Davraz.

Spa and Wellness

As an exercise in nostalgia it's well worth visiting a *hamam*, or Turkish bath – İstanbul in particular boasts many historic hamams worth experiencing for their architecture alone – and, of course, they make for a relaxing end to a day of sightseeing. If you're keen to try one of the famously vigorous massages, the services of a masseur (*tellâk*) are charged extra, or for a less aggressively relaxing treatment, opt for a *kese* session from the masseur: a good scrub with an abrasive mitt.

Throughout Turkey over a thousand hot springs (and some ice-cold ones) bubble their mineral-rich water from deep seismic fissures at high temperature and under great pressure. Roman armies soothed battle wounds in the rich, therapeutic mineral pools. Turkish families have visited the pools and springs for decades and "medical tourism" to take the rejuvenating waters is on an upward curve.

Pamukkale
Page 38

The hot springs at the UNESCO World Heritage Site of Pamukkale have created a geological fairyland of chalk terraces; you can bathe in thermal waters of the sacred pool of the ancients at the nearby ancient site of Hierapolis.

Hamams

Some of the best are the Cağaloğlu Baths in İstanbul (above), the Bodrum Hamam on the Aegean coast and Sefa Hamamı in Antalya – a restored thirteenth-century Selçuki bath.

Five-star treatment

There are a host of five-star, luxury spa hotels across Turkey, offering a mix of relaxation, invigoration and first-class treatments. The greatest concentrations are to be found in and around İstanbul, Ankara and Bodrum.

Retreats

There are retreats and courses of all kinds on offer throughout the country, from yoga, pilates and meditation retreats to shiatsu and assorted "personal growth" breaks.

Bursa

Page 32

One of Turkey's most venerable spa cities; both the New Spa and Old Spa have illustrious histories, dating from the fourteenth and fifteenth centuries.

İstanbul

İstanbul is one of the greatest cities the world has ever known. It has played capital to consecutive Christian and Islamic empires, a role which has shaped the region's history for over 2500 years and bequeathed to İstanbul a staggering wealth of attractions, including the masterpiece of Aya Sofya, the formidable city walls and the domes and minarets of the Ottoman palaces and mosques that dot the city's skyline. These famous sights can be visited in a few days but after that the choices are legion, especially since this youthful city (the average age of İstanbul's citizens is just 23) has reinvented itself as a nightlife, culinary and shopping destination. The only answer is to come back again and again. If you do, this endlessly fascinating city will certainly reward you.

Sultanahmet

Sultanahmet, on the European side of the water, is where most short-stay visitors to İstanbul spend most of their time as it is home to the city's main sightseeing attractions. The monumental architecture, attractive parks and gardens, street-side cafes, and the benefits of a relatively traffic-free main road (courtesy of the tramline) combine to make this area pleasant for sightseeing and as a place to stay during your visit.

> **DID YOU KNOW?**
>
> İstanbul is the only city in the world located on two continents, Europe and Asia. The dividing line is the Bosphorus, the stretch of water which runs between the Black Sea and the Sea of Marmara.

Aya Sofya

For almost a thousand years Aya Sofya, or Hagia Sophia (daily except Mon 9am–7pm, upper galleries close at 6.30pm), was the largest enclosed space in the world and, from its position atop the city's acropolis, it dominated the skyline until the sixteenth century. It was designed to impress both subjects and visiting foreign dignitaries alike and the vast interior – filled with shafts of light from the high windows around the dome – is still an awe-inspiring sight.

The current structure is the third church of the same name – which means "The Church of the Divine Wisdom" – to stand on the site. It was commissioned in the sixth century by Emperor Justinian on a scale unknown to the Byzantine world; no imitation of the enormous thirty-metre dome was attempted until the sixteenth century.

TOPKAPI PALACE

The church was converted to a mosque in 1453, after which the minarets were added; it's been a museum since 1934. There are a few features left over from its time as a mosque: a *mihrab* (niche indicating the direction of Mecca), a *minbar* (pulpit) and the enormous wooden plaques which bear sacred names of God, the Prophet Muhammad and the first four Caliphs. There are also some remains of abstract and figurative mosaics.

Topkapı Palace

Immediately north of Aya Sofya, Topkapı Palace (daily except Tues 9am–7pm, last admission 6pm) is İstanbul's second unmissable sight. Built between 1459 and 1465, the palace was the centre of the Ottoman Empire for nearly four centuries. Past the ticket office is the beautifully restored Divan, containing the Imperial Council Hall. Around the corner is the Harem; the only men once allowed in here were eunuchs and the imperial guardsmen, who were only employed at certain hours and even then blinkered.

The Blue Mosque

With its six minarets, the Sultanahmet Camii, or Blue Mosque (daily 9am–one hour before dusk prayer call), is instantly recognizable; inside, its four "elephant foot" pillars obscure parts of the building and dwarf the dome they support. It's the twenty thousand blue tiles inside that lend the mosque its name. Outside the precinct wall is the Tomb of Sultan Ahmet, where the sultan is buried along with his wife and three of his sons. Behind the mosque is the Vakıf Carpet Museum, which houses antique carpets and kilims from all over Turkey.

Museums

Some of İstanbul's finest museums are located in Sultanahmet. Close to the Blue Mosque the Museum of Turkish and Islamic Art, housed in Ibrahim Paşa's former palace, displays one of the best collections of Islamic artefacts in the world. Just west of the Topkapı Palace you'll find three excellent museums (all May–Sept Tues–Sun

ALEXANDER SARCOPHAGUS, ARCHAEOLOGICAL MUSEUM

9am–6pm; Nov–April Tues–Sun 9am–4pm): in the Archaeological Museum is a superb collection of sarcophagi, sculptures and other remains of past civilizations. The adjacent Çinili Köşk is the oldest secular building in İstanbul, now a Museum of Ceramics housing a select collection of İznik ware and Selçuk tiles. Nearby, the Museum of the Ancient Orient contains a small but dazzling collection of Anatolian, Egyptian and Mesopotamian artefacts.

The city's art scene is thriving as well, with İstanbul Modern in Tophane, around a kilometre from the Galata Bridge, the leading modern gallery. There are a host of other galleries all over İstanbul, showing everything from contemporary art to old masters in venues including converted Ottoman power stations and banks.

The Covered Bazaar

Off the main street of Divan Yolu Caddesi lies the district of Beyazıt, centred on the Kapalı Çarşı or Covered Bazaar (Mon–Sat 8.30am–7.30pm), a huge web of passageways housing more than four thousand shops, each with chatty, persuasive salesmen. Give yourself an hour or two to negotiate its network of alleyways and to soak up the bustling atmosphere. There are carpet shops everywhere catering for all budgets, shops selling leather goods, gold jewellery, slippers, ceramics and mass-made souvenirs.

YEREBATAN SARNICI

Yerebatan Sarnıcı

The Yerebatan Sarnıcı (daily 9am–6.30pm), the "Sunken Palace"
– also known as the Basilica Cistern, was once an integral part of the
Old City's water supply. It's one of several underground cisterns, this
one buried right under the core of Sultanahmet, and the first to have
been extensively excavated. Restored in 1987, the cistern is now
beautifully lit and access made easier by specially constructed
walkways.

Kadıköy

On the Asian (or Anatolian) side of the city, Kadıköy makes a great
day-trip or base for a few days. It's a fun residential district where you
can escape the backpacker hordes of Sultanahmet; many residents live
here and commute to work on the European side. Ferries between the
Asian and European sides are cheap and frequent, take twenty minutes
and operate from around 6am to 11.30pm.

Karaköy and Beyoğlu

Across the Galata Bridge are the districts of Karaköy (formerly Galata) and Beyoğlu. Karaköy was previously the capital's "European" quarter, and has been home to Jewish, Greek and Armenian minorities. Today you'll find boutiques, colourful crafts shops and small art galleries, and it's where locals and clued-up overseas visitors meet in hip café-bars, restaurants and clubs; this is the place to come for a night out without the tourist hordes you get in Sultanahmet. The Galata Tower (daily 9am–7pm), built in 1348, is the area's most obvious landmark; its viewing

ISTIKLAL CADDESI, BEYOĞLU

GALATA TOWER

galleries, café and expensive restaurant offer the best panoramas of the city.

Up towards Istiklâl Caddesi, Beyoğlu's main boulevard, an unassuming doorway leads to the courtyard of the Galata Mevlevihane (9am–4.30pm, closed Wed), a former monastery and ceremonial hall of the Whirling Dervishes, a sect founded in the thirteenth century. Staged dervish ceremonies take place at the Sirkeci Central Train Station Exhibition Hall (check at the Mevlevihane for details). Pay a visit to the Pera Museum (Tues–Sat 10am–7pm; Sun noon–6pm) on Meşrutiyet Cad 65, housed in a beautiful nineteenth-century building and displaying changing exhibitions of contemporary art, historical oil paintings of old İstanbul, ceramic tiles and a collection of old weights and measures.

The Sea of Marmara

Despite their proximity to İstanbul, the shores and hinterland of the Sea of Marmara are relatively neglected by foreign travellers – but there are good reasons to come: not least the former Ottoman capitals of Edirne and Bursa, the latter of which has some of the finest monuments in the Balkans.

Two particularly bright spots on the Thracian coast are the beach-and-fortress town of Kıyıköy on the Black Sea and the Saros Gulf resort of Erikli. For evocative scenery inland, the Uludağ range above Bursa is popular with skiers in winter and hikers in summer.

SELİMİYE CAMİİ

Edirne

Bordering both Greece and Bulgaria, the small town of Edirne boasts an impressive number of elegant monuments. It's a sleepy place for most of the year but the town really springs to life for the week-long oil-wrestling festival of Kırkpınar at the end of June (see box opposite).

The Eski Camii is the oldest mosque in town; begun in 1403 it uses recycled Roman pillars and is famed for its giant calligraphic inscriptions inside. Just across the way, the

Bedesten was Edirne's first covered market. The beautiful **Üç Şerefeli Camii** mosque dates from 1447 and has four idiosyncratic minarets, the tallest of which has three galleries for the muezzin. A little way east of here, the masterly **Selimiye Camii** was designed by Mimar Sinan. Its four slender minarets, among the tallest in the world, also have three balconies; the interior is most impressive, its dome planned to surpass that of Aya Sofya in İstanbul.

Kıyıköy

Kıyıköy occupies an idyllic location overlooking the Black Sea, flanked on both sides by slow-moving rivers and lushly forested spurs of the Istranca hills. Crumbling half-timbered houses line the backstreets and fishing nets hang all around.

OIL WRESTLING

Oil-wrestling (*yağlı güreş*) is popular throughout Turkey, but reaches the pinnacle of acclaim at the annual **Kırkpınar festival**, staged each summer on the islet of Sarayiçi close to Edirne. Tradition still permeates the event: the contestants – up to a thousand come from all  over Turkey – dress only in leather breeches called *kisbet* and are slicked down head-to-toe in diluted olive oil. The bouts can last anything from a few minutes to nearly an hour, until one competitor collapses or has his back pinned to the grass.

Aya Nikola Manastırı is an elaborate structure carved into the rock of the hillside, complete with colonnaded aisles and barrel vaulting. A fifteen-minute walk west of the village takes you to 2km of pristine sandy **beach**, backed by low cliffs oozing fossils. Several more almost empty beaches – some of the most beautiful and undeveloped in Turkey – lie east of Kıyıköy, near where the Pabuçdere meets the sea.

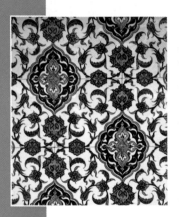

İznik

A day or overnight trip from Bursa or İstanbul is enough to see the main sights of **İznik** (ancient Nicaea) and pick up a souvenir or two from the local ceramics workshops. In its sixteenth-century heyday, İznik produced Turkey's best tiles, and the tradition has been recently revived here.

In the northeast quadrant is a vast, landscaped park, dotted with İznik's most famous monuments: the **Yeşil Camii**, or Green Mosque, is a small gem of a building; and the fourteenth-century **Nilüfer Hatun İmareti** now contains the **İznik Museum**, where artefacts from the town's chequered history are on display. You won't be able to miss the double **town walls**, and if time permits, a walk or drive up to the nearby **Abdülvahap hill** affords fine views over İznik and its surroundings.

Çanakkale

Çanakkale is a progressive, modern city, celebrated for its setting on the Dardanelles, and is a popular base for visiting Gelibolu (Gallipoli; see below) and Troy. There's a big university here and the fifteen thousand students, together with Aussie and Kiwi backpackers, make for a busy nightlife scene and you'll find no shortage of bars, clubs and places to eat. The park, Naval Museum (Tues, Wed & Fri–Sun 9am–noon & 1.30–5pm) and Archaeological Museum (daily 8am–noon & 1–5.30pm) make interesting visits, plus you might recognize the wooden Trojan horse on the seafront promenade from the 2004 film *Troy*.

TROJAN HORSE IN ÇANAKKALE

The Gelibolu (Gallipoli) Peninsula

Though endowed with splendid scenery and beaches, the slender Gelibolu (Gallipoli) peninsula is known chiefly for its grim military history. In April 1915 it was the site of a plan to land Allied troops with a view to putting Turkey out of the war. Huge strategic mistakes, as well as a fierce opposition headed by the gifted officer Mustafa Kemal (Atatürk), led to the dismal failure of the operation, incurring massive casualties.

MEHMETÇİK MEMORIAL, GALLIPOLI

Tours – by turns moving and numbing – are likely to
include the Kabatepe Orientation Centre and Museum
(daily 8am–6pm), Shrapnel Valley and Shell Green
cemeteries, followed by ANZAC Cove and Arıburnu, site of
the ANZAC landing and Conkbayırı Hill.

Bursa

Draped along the leafy lower slopes of Uludağ, which
towers more than 2000m above, Bursa – first capital of the
Ottoman Empire – houses some of the finest early
Ottoman monuments in Turkey, in a tidy and appealing
city centre.

The interior of the fourteenth-century mosque, Ulu
Camii, is dominated by a huge şadırvan – a fountain and
pool for ritual ablutions – and it's worth looking out for
the spectacular Yeşil Camii (daily 8am–8.30pm) and Yeşil

BURSA'S COCOON AUCTION

The highlight of the Bursa bazaar's year is the cocoon auction in late June and early July, when silk-breeders from around the province gather to hawk their valuable produce; during the auction the courtyard floor of the Koza Hanı becomes a lake of white torpedoes the size of a songbird's egg.

Türbe (daily 8am–noon & 1–7pm) mosques as well. Just north of Ulu Camii, the city's covered market, the Bedesten, is given over to the sale of jewellery and precious metals.

West of the centre, the Hisar ("citadel") district was Bursa's original nucleus. Narrow lanes wind up past dilapidated Ottoman houses, while walkways clinging to the rock face offer fabulous views.

Uludağ

Presiding over Bursa, 2543-metre-high Uludağ ("Great Mountain") is a dramatic massif, its northern reaches dropping precipitously into the city. A cable car (*teleferik*) links Bursa with the popular Sarıalan picnic grounds at 1635m. A few hours' walking to the east (outside the National Park) will bring you to some glacial lakes in a wild, rocky setting just below the highest summit. Skiing is possible from December to March, though it's better earlier in the season than later.

THE SEA OF MARMARA | 33

The Aegean Coast

The Aegean coast is, in many ways, Turkey's most enticing destination, home to some of the best of its antiquities and the most appealing resorts. İzmir serves as a base for day-trips to nearby sights and beaches. Visitors continuing south will be spoilt for sightseeing choices as the territory is rich in Classical, Hellenistic and Roman ruins, notably Ephesus, Pergamon and the remains inland at Hierapolis – sitting atop the famous pools and mineral formations of Pamukkale. Although some of the larger beach resorts are overdeveloped for some people's taste, Bodrum retains a real charm and is the seaside holiday spot of choice for holidaymakers from the capital.

İzmir

İzmir – ancient Smyrna – is a booming, cosmopolitan and relentlessly modern place. Visitors are likely to spend most time in the Konak area, marked by the ornate Saat Kulesi (clock tower), the city's official symbol. Head north and you'll reach the Kültür Parkı, a large park with regular outdoor entertainment. Continue in the same direction and you'll soon reach the district of Alsancak – the hub of evening entertainment with alfresco bars and restaurants. The city's free elevator, Asansör, a twenty-minute walk south, offers wonderful views over the city and Gulf of İzmir.

> **DID YOU KNOW?**
>
> The word *meze* – the tempting and varied platters served up across Turkey – comes from the Arabic *mezza*, meaning "taste" or "sample".

The Archaeological Museum (Tues–Sun 9am–noon & 1–5pm) displays some stunning finds from all over İzmir province and next door is the charming Ethnography Museum (Tues–Sun 9am–noon & 1–5pm) where you can learn about the local tradition of camel wrestling and see examples of Anatolian crafts. Finally, the castle ruins of Kadifekale (always open, and a short bus ride from Konak) provide great views of İzmir's metropolitan expanse.

Kuşadası

Kuşadası is Turkey's most established resort, and a popular stop on cruise ship itineraries. The most famous of its beaches is Kadınlar Denizi, 3km southwest of town, which can be crowded in season; much the best in the area is Pamucak, 15km north, an exposed 4km stretch of sand that is as yet little developed. Kuşadası's old town also has its charms even when the centre is thronged with visitors. The Kale district, huddled inside the town walls, is the oldest and most appealing part of town, with a mosque and some fine traditional houses.

KUŞADASI MARINA

Ephesus

With the exception of Pompeii, Ephesus (*Efes* in Turkish) is the largest and best-preserved ancient city around the Mediterranean. It's understandably popular; your best hope of avoiding the crowds is to visit early morning. The nearby town of Selçuk, an easy twenty-minute walk from the site, makes an excellent base for visiting the ruins.

Originally situated close to a temple devoted to the goddess Artemis, Ephesus' location by a fine harbour was the secret of its success in ancient times, eventually making it the wealthy capital of Roman Asia, ornamented with magnificent public buildings.

In the centre of the site (daily 8am–5.30pm) is the Arcadian Way, which was once lined with hundreds of

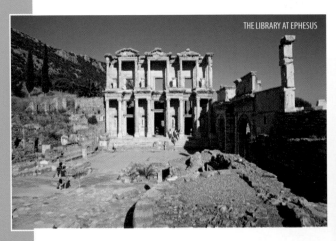

THE LIBRARY AT EPHESUS

shops and illuminated at night. The
nearby theatre has been partly restored
to allow its use for open-air concerts
and occasional summer festivals; climb
to the top for views of the surrounding
countryside. Across the intersection
looms the elegant Library of Celsus,
erected by the consul Gaius Julius
Aquila between 110 and 135 AD. Just

uphill, a Byzantine fountain looks across the Street of the Curetes to
the public latrines, a favourite with visitors. Official guides to the
site can be booked via the tourist office in town and should have a
tourist guide license from the Ministry of Culture and Tourism.

Şirince

Another pleasant day-trip from Selçuk is the pretty hillside village
of Şirince. Despite being overrun with tourist buses the village is
stunning, full of nineteenth-century houses lining higgledy-
piggledy, steep cobbled passageways. Spending a night here is a
treat, as long as you like peace and quiet; there's little in the way
of nightlife here.

Bodrum

In the eyes of its devotees, Bodrum – ancient Halicarnassus – with its
whitewashed houses and subtropical gardens, is the most attractive
Turkish resort, a quality outfit in comparison to its upstart Aegean rivals.
The town's centrepiece is the Castle of St Peter (Tues–Sun 9am–noon &
1–5pm; summer open until 7pm), built by the Knights of St John

between 1437 and 1522. Inside, the various towers house a fascinating Museum of Underwater Archaeology, which includes coin and jewellery rooms, Classical and Hellenistic statuary, and Byzantine relics retrieved from various wrecks. Some displays may be closed without warning, though you can always bank on enjoying the fantastic views of the water from various vantage points in the castle. Immediately north of the castle lies the bazaar, from where you can stroll up to Türkkuyusu Caddesi to see what's left of the Mausoleum (Tues–Sun 8.30am–5.30pm), the burial place of Mausolus, ruler of Halicarnassos from 376–353 BC and the origin of the word mausoleum.

Pamukkale

The rock formations of Pamukkale (literally "Cotton Castle"), 140km northeast of Marmaris, are the most-visited attraction in this part of Turkey, a series of white terraces saturated with dissolved calcium bicarbonate, bubbling up from the feet of the Çal Dağı mountains beyond. The spring emerges in what was once the ancient

PAMUKKALE

city of Hierapolis, the ruins of which would merit a stop even if they weren't coupled with the natural phenomenon. Up on the plateau you can bathe in "the sacred pool of the ancients" (daily 8am–6.30pm; 25TL), in the 35°C mineral water.

Hierapolis

The archaeological zone of Hierapolis lies behind the Pamukkale terraces. Its main features include a Temple of Apollo and the infamous, albeit inconspicuous, plutonium cavern, where a toxic mixture of sulphur dioxide and carbon dioxide brews (the site is now firmly out of bounds). Perhaps the most interesting part of the city is the colonnaded street which once extended for almost 1km, terminating in monumental portals a few paces outside the walls – of which only the most northerly, a triple arch, still stands.

The Mediterranean Coast

The first stretch of Turkey's Mediterranean coast, dominated by the **Akdağ** and **Bey** mountain ranges of the Taurus chain and known as the "**Turquoise Coast**", is its most popular, famed for its pine-studded shore, minor ruins and beautiful scenery. In the west, **Fethiye** is a perfect base for vişits to **Ölüdeniz**, **Kaya Köyü** and **Butterfly Valley**. The scenery becomes increasingly spectacular as you head towards the site of **Olympos**, and **Kaş**, which offers great scuba-diving and adventure sports.

ÖLÜDENIZ

Fethiye

Fethiye is well sited for access to some of the region's ancient sites, many of which date from the time when this area was the independent kingdom of Lycia. The best beaches, around the **Ölüdeniz lagoon** (Ölüdeniz means "dead sea" in Turkish), are now very crowded but Fethiye itself has been able to spread to accommodate increased tourist traffic.

Fethiye occupies the site of the Lycian city of Telmessos, little of which remains other than the impressive **ancient theatre**, and a number of Lycian **rock tombs** on the hillside. You can also visit the remains of the **medieval fortress** behind the harbour area of town. In the centre of town the small museum (Tues–Sun 8.30am–5pm) has some fascinating exhibits from local sites. Numerous boats on the harbour offer island-hopping trips.

Kaya Köyü and Ölüdeniz

One of the most dramatic sights in the area is the ghost village of **Kaya Köyü** (Levissi). The village was abandoned in 1923, when its Anatolian-Greek population was relocated, and all you see now is a hillside covered with more than two thousand ruined cottages and an attractive basilica. **Ölüdeniz** is about two hours on foot from Kaya Köyü or a dolmuş ride from Fethiye. The warm waters of this lagoon make for pleasant swimming although the crowds can reach saturation level in high season – in which case the nearby beaches of Belceğiz and Kıdrak are better bets.

BUTTERFLY VALLEY

Butterfly Valley

Popularized in the 1980s by hippies, **Butterfly Valley** (*Kelebek Vadisi*) is a peaceful spot to spend a couple of days. Reached by boat from Ölüdeniz, it's home to a colony of butterflies, including the Jersey Tiger. Lazy days drift into a cycle of sleeping, eating, swimming and night-time campfires.

Kaş and Kalkan

Kaş is beautifully located, nestled in a small curving bay below rocky cliffs. But what was once a sleepy fishing village is fast becoming an **adventure sports** centre, with nightlife to match, and provides a handy base for paragliding, mountain biking and some of the cheapest and best scuba-diving in Turkey. Scattered around the streets and to the west are the remains of ancient **Antiphellos**, one of the few Lycian cities to bear a Greek name. The town is also well situated for the nearby ruins of Kekova and Patara.

SCUBA-DIVING AROUND KAŞ

The Mediterranean around Kaş has arguably the best visibility and greatest variety of sea life along the entire Turkish coast; you're likely to spot grouper, barracuda, amberjack, garfish, ray, wrasse, bream and parrotfish, among a host of other species. There are nearly sixty dive sites in the area, many along the Çukurbağ peninsula, with most others around the islets at the marine frontier with Kastellórizo.

Twenty-five kilometres up the coast is the village of **Kalkan**. It developed a rather bohemian atmosphere in the 1980s and has since become a haven for expats – 1500 of the 4000 inhabitants are from abroad, mostly British. This pretty fishing village is a great place to stay if you want to explore Patara and Xanthos, ancient capital of the Lycian League, or the inland mountain settlements of Islamlar and Bezirgan.

Olympos and Çıralı

The Lycian site of **Olympos** is located in an idyllic location on a beautiful sandy bay and the banks of a largely dry river. You can while away several hours rambling among the striking overgrown ruins

– including Byzantine tombs, a bath-house, a canal, churches, and mosaics – before chilling out on the beach.

A 1.5km walk along the pebbly beach is the quieter holiday village of Çıralı. About an hour's well-marked stroll above the village's citrus groves flickers the dramatic **Chimaera** (open 24hr), a series of naturally-occurring eternal flames issuing from cracks in the bare rock, particularly beautiful at night.

Antalya

Antalya is blessed with an ideal climate and a stunning setting and the old town in particular is an agreeable place to spend some time. The town is dominated by the **Yivli Minare** or "Fluted Minaret", erected in the thirteenth century. Downhill from here is the **old harbour**, recently restored and site of the evening promenade. In the atmospheric **Kaleiçi** ("old town"), every house is now a carpet shop, café or *pansiyon*. The one thing you shouldn't

RAFTING IN KÖPRÜLÜ CANYON, NEAR ANTALYA

miss is **Antalya Museum** (Tues–Sun 9am– 6.30pm), one of the top five archaeological collections in the country.

Aspendos

Antalya's principal attraction, the Roman theatre of Aspendos – one of the best preserved in Turkey – is situated on the outskirts of the city. The theatre is pretty much exactly as spectators would have seen it during the theatre's heyday, a state of preservation due in part to Atatürk who, after a visit, declared that it should be preserved and used for performances rather than as a museum. This started a tradition which flourishes today in the **Aspendos Opera and Ballet Festival** (see box).

OPERA AT THE THEATRE OF ASPENDOS

Central Turkey

When the first Turkish nomads arrived in Anatolia during the tenth and eleventh centuries, the landscape must have been strongly reminiscent of their Central Asian homeland. **Ankara** grew as a result of immigration from the Anatolian villages to become the metropolis it is now. The south-central part of the country draws more visitors, not least for **Cappadocia** in the far east of the region, where water and wind have created a land of fantastic forms from the soft tufa rock, including forests of cones, table mountains and canyon-like valleys. Further south still, **Konya** is best known as the birthplace of the mystical Sufi sect and makes an interesting place to stop over between Cappadocia and the coast.

CAVE DWELLINGS IN CAPPADOCIA

Ankara

Modern **Ankara** is really two cities, a double identity due to the breakneck pace at which it has developed since being declared capital of the Turkish Republic in 1923. The old city is a village of narrow cobbled streets and ramshackle wooden houses centring on the **Hisar**, Ankara's fortress and citadel. Inside its confines you'll find **Ak Kale**, a castle ruin which provides perfect views over the city. The **Museum of Anatolian Civilizations** (Tues–Sun 9am–5.30pm) boasts an incomparable collection of archaeological objects housed in a restored Ottoman *Bedesten*, or covered market.

To the south, the districts of **Kızılay**, **Kavaklıdere** and **Çankaya** are some of the most popular in the city for entertainment, bars and restaurants. Kızılay maintains a bohemian air and aspiring authors sell and sign their books on street corner, while Kavaklıdere and Çankaya are good choices for more contemporary venues.

The Hittite Sites

Around 120km east of Ankara, centred on the village of Boğazkale, are the most impressive and significant **Hittite sites** in Anatolia. This area was once the heart of the Hittite Empire and **Hattuşa**, spread over several square kilometres to the south of the modern village, was its capital. You can still see the limestone foundation blocks from the buildings of this once-vast city, spread over a steeply sloping hillside, dotted with rocky outcrops. A few kilometres to the east is the temple site of **Yazılıkaya**, while **Alacahöyük**, a smaller Hittite settlement dating back to 4000 BC, 25km north of Boğazkale, is further off the beaten track.

Amasya

Blessed with a super-abundant historical legacy, and occupying a river valley so narrow that it's almost a gorge, **Amasya** is one of the high points of the region. Most people come to see the rock tombs hewn into the cliffs above the town by the kings of Pontus over two thousand years ago, but Amasya also harbours some truly beautiful Selçuk and Ottoman architecture, and a multitude of colourful nineteenth-century wooden houses. A great number of these have been superbly restored, many reopening as authentic and atmospheric antique shops, guesthouses and restaurants.

Derinkuyu

The most thoroughly excavated of the region's underground cities is **Derinkuyu** (daily 8am–5.30pm), 29km from Nevşehir. The city is well lit, and the original ventilation system still functions remarkably well, though some of the passages are small and cramped. The excavated area (only a quarter of the total) consists of eight levels and includes stables, wine presses and a dining hall or schoolroom with two long, rock-cut tables, plus a cruciform church and dungeon.

Konya

Konya is a place of pilgrimage for the Muslim world – the home of Celalledin Rumi or the Mevlâna ("Our Master"), the mystic who founded the Mevlevî or Whirling Dervish sect, and the centre of Sufic mystical practice and teaching.

The **Mevlâna Museum** (Mon 10am–5pm, Tues–Sun 9am–5pm) is housed in the first lodge (*tekke*) of the Mevlevî dervish sect, recognizable by its distinctive fluted turquoise dome. The museum holds the mausoleum containing the tombs of the Mevlâna, his father and other notables as well as displays of musical instruments and a 500-year-old silk carpet from Selçuk Persia that is supposedly the finest ever woven. Another attraction is the **Karatay Tile Museum**; the interior of the thirteenth-century building (daily 8am–noon & 1–5pm) is as fascinating as the ceramics on show, with a beautifully decorated domed central ceiling and ornamental green tiles.

WHIRLING DERVISHES

Cappadocia

The unique landscape of Cappadocia is now one of the star attractions of Turkey. A land created by the complex interaction of natural and human forces over vast spans of time, it is a superlative visual experience. Its weird formations of soft, volcanic rock have been adapted into caves and even underground cities over centuries by many cultures.

Within the region between Nevşehir, Avanos and Ürgüp are the greater part of the valleys of **fairy chimneys**, the **rock-cut churches** of the **Göreme Open-Air Museum** with their beautiful frescoes, and the **Zelve monastery**, a fascinating warren of troglodyte dwellings and churches. **Nevşehir**, largest of the towns, is an important hub for travel in the region, while **Ürgüp** and its neighbouring villages, Göreme, Çavuşin, Üçhisar and Ortahisar, all make attractive bases from which to tour the surrounding valleys. **Avanos**, beautifully situated on the Kızılırmak River, is a centre of the local pottery industry.

Outside this main area are the underground cities of **Derinkuyu** and **Kaymaklı**, fascinating warrens attesting to the ingenuity of the ancient inhabitants. Less well-known sites are located further to the south, east and west. The **Ihlara valley** near Aksaray, a red canyon riddled with churches cut into its sides, is the most spectacular sight yet to feel the full force of tourism. **Kayseri** has long been a quiet provincial capital, recommended for its Selçuk architecture and bazaars, and side trips out to the ski resort on **Erciyes Dağı** and the Sultansazlığı bird sanctuary (see box, p.48). To the south, attractions around the town of Niğde include the Eski Gümüşler monastery, whose frescoes rival the more famous examples in Göreme.

BALLOONING OVER CAPPADOCIA

The region's canyons and fairy chimneys take on a whole new aspect when viewed from above, and hot-air-balloon trips are now incredibly popular. Check what your itinerary will include before booking, but a flight is sure to take you over the fairy chimneys for some breathtaking views. Göreme and Çavuşin are good places to find reputable companies.

Eastern Turkey

Relatively few travellers make it to Turkey's eastern regions, but many of those who do find it the most stimulating part of the country. In the northeast you'll find outdoor activities in abundance, from whitewater rafting to hiking and mountaineering, alongside archaeological sites and historical monuments. To the south, the basin of the Euphrates and Tigris rivers is the most exotic part of Turkey, offering a heady mix of middle-eastern atmosphere and evocative ancient sites; the mountain-top funerary sanctuary of Nemrut Dağı is a particular highlight. In the remote southeast, the land takes on an austere natural beauty, dominated by soaring peaks, rugged plateaux and plunging valleys, with the vast inland sea of Lake Van and graceful volcanic cone of Mount Ararat (*Ağrı Dağı*) at its heart.

MOUNT ARARAT

The Georgian valleys

GEORGIAN RUINS

Turkey's far northeast was once under the command of the Georgian kingdom and, despite centuries of Ottoman rule, evidence of this historical legacy remains tangible; simply driving through a landscape strewn with ruined castles and churches – some perched on seemingly inaccessible hilltops – is an experience in itself

To the north of Erzurum, the area's largest urban base, lie the southern valleys, the highlights of which are the churches of Haho and Öşk Vank. Those without their own transport will find it easier to tour the western valleys from the main town, Yusufeli, which also provides a good base from which to organize a tour of the Kaçkar Dağları, one of Turkey's most stunning mountain ranges.

The Armenian ruins

Centuries of Armenian rule have also left their mark in eastern Turkey with a series of superb ruins, whose remains pepper the modern-day border. Many find this area even more scenic than that housing the Georgian ruins: think lofty, rolling fields instead of crinkle-cut valleys. You're almost certain to pass through the attractive city of Kars, the area's main city, especially if you're on your way to Ani, justifiably the

SKIING AT PALANDÖKEN

Palandöken, 5–6.5km south of Erzurum, offers far and away the best skiing in Turkey, with reliably excellent conditions in the chill winters. Pistes total 35km at present with 10km more projected, with nine lifts in total giving access to eight easy runs, six intermediate and two advanced, plus four recognized off-piste routes.

best-known complex in the area. Once the Armenian capital, it is now mainly an expanse of rubble but it retains an isolated, decaying grandeur carrying subtle echoes of former glories. Also in the area are the complexes of Karmir Vank and Horomos and, further afield, the churches at Khtskonk and Mren.

The Kaçkar Dağları

A formidable barrier between the northeastern Anatolian plateau and the Black Sea, the Kaçkar Dağları (Kaçkar Mountains) are the high end of the Pontic coastal ranges and Turkey's most rewarding and popular trekking area. They are not the highest peaks in the country but in scenic and human interest they fully earn their aliases "the Little Caucasus" and "the Pontic Alps".

KAÇKAR DAĞLARI

The six most popular trailhead villages are – on the Black Sea slopes – Çat and Ayder, and on the Çoruh side Barhal, Hevek, Meretet and Tekkale. The gradients tend to be gentler from the Black Sea side, but an almost daily mist and busier tracks can be a problem in the main June–September season. Many visitors spend a week or more in the region, taking in the beauty of the surroundings and the fascinating patchwork of tribes that inhabit the hills.

Nemrut Dağı

The remote, grandiose mountain-top sanctuary at Nemrut Dağı (Mount Nemrut) is unforgettable and the mighty stone heads adorning the temple and tomb of King Antiochus I have become some of the best-known images of eastern Turkey. Antiochus was the last ruler of the short-lived Commagene dynasty, which would merit no more than a footnote in the region's history were it not for the king's exceptional vanity. In building this colossal monument to himself, he hoped to guarantee eternal life and prove his faith in the gods. The five, much-photographed, detached heads represent Antiochus I, Fortuna, Zeus, Apollo and Hercules. Tour groups

NEMRUT DAĞI

tend to arrive in time for either sunrise or sunset for the beautiful light, though a visit during the warmer daytime can allow you to explore in relative peace and quiet.

Gaziantep

The rapidly expanding city of Gaziantep draws you in through a fascinating history, having been occupied by Hittites, Assyrians, Persians, Alexandrines, Romans, Selçuks, Byzantines and Arabs. Its prize asset is the Zeugma Archaeological Museum (Tues–Sun 8am–noon & 1–5pm), which holds the finest collection of mosaics in Turkey, including 800 square metres rescued from the Hellenistic/Roman border city of Zeugma. In culinary terms, the city is also unrivalled for its sweets, particularly pistachio-based pastries like baklava and fıstık sarma.

Mardin and Harran

Seen from the south, Mardin looks spectacular, its tiered layers of vernacular houses, mansions, mosques and churches clinging to a huge citadel-topped rock, rising out of the plain. It is the main hub for tourism in southeast Turkey and boasts excellent accommodation and facilities for the visitors.

The beehive-style houses of Harran are an established attraction in the region. The town has been continuously inhabited for 6000 years and has strong biblical connections. The distinctive houses – mud-covered stone buildings – are now more commonly used as stores or livestock habitations.

Van and Lake Van

The city of Van is rapidly transforming itself into a modern, buzzing city, and is a great base to explore the area. Van Kalesi ("the rock of Van") is the main local point of interest – an Urartian fortification occupying a narrow outcrop 3km west of the city. Other sites in the region include the Armenian island church of Akdamar, the ruined palace Çavuştepe, and the well-preserved remains of the monastery church of St John at Çarpanak.

The vast expanse of Lake Van, at almost four thousand square kilometres virtually an inland sea, is one of the most unusual features of eastern Turkey. It's a magnet for serious bird-watchers as it lies on the main migration route to Africa.

AKDAMAR ISLAND, LAKE VAN

The Black Sea Coast

Extending from just east of İstanbul to the frontier with Georgia, the Black Sea region is an anomaly, guaranteed to smash any stereotypes held about Turkey. The combined action of damp northerly and westerly winds, and an almost uninterrupted wall of mountains south of the shore, has created a relentlessly rainy and riotously green realm.

Amasra and the western coast

If you have your own transport, travelling around the little-visited western portion of the Black Sea coast can be immensely rewarding, with smooth roads, quiet coves, long beaches and sleepy villages strung out from Sinop to Amasra.

BOZTEPE, AMASRA

Amasra itself is bathed in history, but the modern town is a quiet place during the day, full of shady corners to sit and contemplate; by night it's much livelier and the old walls are lit up attractively, though it doesn't lose its small-town charm.

The main town and the island of Boztepe (across a narrow stone bridge) are scattered with ancient fortifications from two Byzantine/Genoese castles near the tip of the peninsula.

Ordu

The old houses of the small city of Ordu – called Kotorya by the ancients – scale the green slopes of Boztepe to the west, above the recently restored nineteenth century Greek Orthodox cathedral. There are other interesting historic remnants in the local museum in the Paşaoğlu Konaği.

Trabzon

No other Turkish city except İstanbul has exercised such a hold on the Western imagination as Trabzon (ancient Trebizond). Travel writers from Marco Polo to Rose Macaulay have been enthralled by the fabulous image of this quasi-mythical metropolis. Today the celebrated gilded roofs and cosmopolitan texture of Trebizond are long gone but a little poke around the cobbled alleyways will unearth tangible evidence of its former splendour – not least the monastic church of Aya Sofya, home to some of the most outstanding Byzantine frescoes in Anatolia. The atmospheric old town is well worth a visit, too; in the best preserved parts its crenellated walls give an idea of Trabzon's skyline in its heyday.

The Monastery of Sumela

The spectacularly situated Monastery of Sumela was the most prestigious of many that sprang up in the mountains behind Trabzon in the Byzantine era. A monastery has existed on the site since the fourth century, though most of the current structure dates from the thirteenth and fourteenth centuries. Despite decay and vandalism to the former living quarters, a myriad of frescoes still cover almost every surface within the principal shrines, with some of the earliest and best dating from the fourteenth and fifteenth centuries. If you tire of craning your neck to look at the art works, there's always the stunning view over the valley, and the opportunity to imagine what monastic life must have been like here in Sumela's prime.

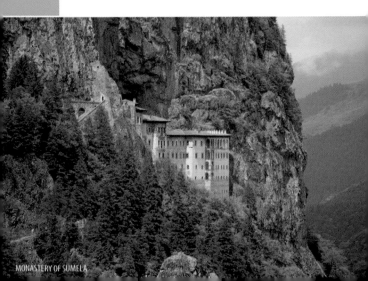

The Hemşin valleys

The most scenic and interesting of the foothill regions east of Trabzon are the valleys of the Fırtına Çayı and its tributaries, which tumble off the steepest slopes of the Pontic ranges, here known as the Kaçkar Dağları (see p.54). Between the mountains and the sea lie a few hundred square kilometres of rugged, isolated territory known simply as Hemşin.

UPPER FIRTINA VALLEY

The upper Fırtına valley

Above the town of Şenyuva, along the main branch of the Fırtına Çayı, the road steadily worsens while the scenery just as relentlessly becomes more spectacular. Some 12.5km from Çamlıhemşin, the single-towered castle of Zilkale, improbably sited by either the Byzantines or the Genoese to control a decidedly minor trade route, appears at a bend in the track. The tree-tufted ruin, more often than not garnished with wisps of mist, today dominates nothing more than one of the most evocative settings in the Pontus.

Practical Information

Money

Turkey's currency is the **Türk Lirası** or **TL** for short, subdivided into 100 *kuruş*. At the time of writing the **exchange rate** was around 2.20TL to the euro, 2.80TL to the pound and 1.8TL to the US dollar. Rates for foreign currency are always better inside Turkey. It's wise to bring a fair wad of **hard currency** with you; euros are particularly useful.

The best exchange rate is usually given by **state-owned banks** (try Ziraat Bankası or Halk Bankası), but queues can be long. **Döviz**, or exchange houses, are common in cities and resorts; they keep longer hours than the banks but often charge commission and offer lower rates.

Credit cards are now widely used in hotels, shops, restaurants, travel agencies and entertainment venues and with no commission (though many hotels and shops offer discounts for cash payments). Swipe readers plus **chip-and-PIN** protocol are now the norm in most of Turkey. There is a widespread **ATM** network. Most bank ATMs will accept any debit cards that are part of the Cirrus, Maestro or Visa/Plus systems. You can also use Visa or MasterCard to get cash from ATMs, though American Express card holders are currently restricted to those of Akbank and Vakıf.

Internet

Many hotels, pensions and even hostels in tourist areas have **internet access** – often both terminals and wi-fi signal, as do an ever-increasing number of cafés. In more remote places in the interior, and the east of the country, only the more expensive hotels have wi-fi.

Mail

Post offices are easily spotted by their bold black-on-yellow **PTT** (Posta, Telegraf, Telefon) signs. Stamps are only available from the PTT, whose website (ⓦwww.ptt.gov.tr) has a (not necessarily up-to-date) English-language listing of services and prices. Post offices are generally open Mon–Fri 8.30am–5.30pm and until noon on Saturday. Delivery to Europe or North America can take seven to ten days. A pricier express (*acele*) service is also available, which cuts delivery times to EU countries to about three days.